# iScience
## Readers

W9-BCJ-189

# Trees:
## Worlds Within Leaves

## by Emily Sohn and Karen J. Rothbardt

Chief Content Consultant
Edward Rock
Associate Executive Director, National Science Teachers Association

NORWOOD HOUSE PRESS
Chicago, IL

Norwood House Press
PO Box 316598
Chicago, IL 60631

For information regarding Norwood House Press, please visit our website at www.norwoodhousepress.com or call 866-565-2900.

Special thanks to: Amanda Jones, Amy Karasick, Alanna Mertens, Terrence Young, Jr.

Editors: Barbara J. Foster, Diane C. Hinckley
Designer: Daniel M. Greene
Production Management: Victory Productions

**Library of Congress Cataloging-in-Publication data**

Sohn, Emily.

    Trees: worlds within leaves / by Emily Sohn and Karen Rothbardt.
    p. cm.

    Summary: "Describes what different kinds of trees need to survive and explains that plants, animals and even humans need trees to survive. As readers use scientific inquiry to learn about what makes each kind of tree unique, an activity based on real world situations challenges them to apply what they've learned in order to solve a puzzle"—Provided by publisher.

Includes bibliographical references and index.

ISBN-13: 978-1-59953-411-4 (library edition: alk. paper)
ISBN-10: 1-59953-411-8 (library edition: alk. paper)

1. Trees—Juvenile literature. I. Rothbardt, Karen. II. Title.

QK475.8.S64 2011
582.16—dc22
         2010044535

Manufactured in the United States of America in North Mankato, Minnesota.

165N—012011

# Contents

**Note to Caregivers:**

Throughout this book, many questions are posed to the reader. Some are open-ended and ask what the reader thinks. Discuss these questions with your child and guide him or her in thinking through the possible answers and outcomes. There are also questions posed which have a specific answer. Encourage your child to read through the text to determine the correct answer. Most importantly, encourage answers grounded in reality while also allowing imaginations to soar. Information to help support you as you share the book with your child is provided in the back in the **Additional Notes** section.

Words that are **bolded** are defined in the glossary in the back of the book.

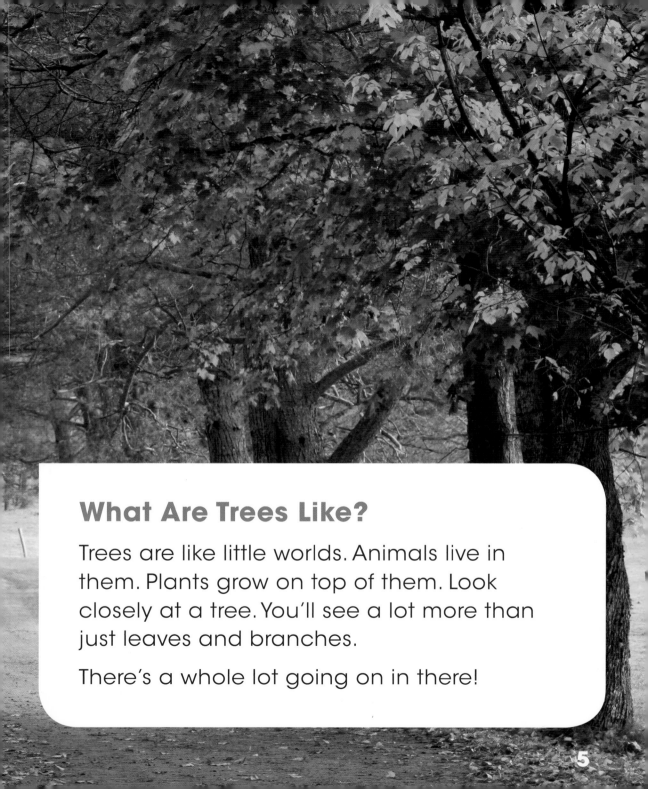

## What Are Trees Like?

Trees are like little worlds. Animals live in them. Plants grow on top of them. Look closely at a tree. You'll see a lot more than just leaves and branches.

There's a whole lot going on in there!

# Which Tree Is Right for Your Tree House?

You and your friend want a tree house in the woods. You need to decide which tree will be best to build it in. In this wooded area, there are four types of trees: an oak, a willow, a maple, and a pine. Which tree will you choose?

 **Choice 1: Oak Tree**

 **Choice 2: Willow Tree**

 **Choice 3: Maple Tree**

**Choice 4: Pine Tree**

Here are some things to think about:

1. Is the tree strong enough to hold your tree house?

2. Does the tree have a good shape to fit a tree house?

3. Do insects live in this kind of tree? What else might make this tree a bad place to stay in?

4. Does the tree drop nuts, fruits, or even branches?

## What Are the Parts of a Tree?

What is the best tree to put your tree house in? To find out, grab a pencil and a notebook. Now, go outside. Find a park or a street with trees on it. Draw as many of the trees as you can.

Now, look at your pictures. How are the trees alike? How are they different? Where would you put a tree house in each one?

You know a tree when you see one. That's because all trees share some things in common. Here are some parts that every tree has: leaves, branches, trunks, and **roots.** How else are trees alike?

# How Can You Describe Trees?

Trees are like people. No two are exactly the same. Oak and maple trees have wide leaves. They also have thick, stiff branches. But willow trees have thin leaves. They also have thin, bendy branches.

Would you rather climb an oak tree or a willow tree? Remember: You will have to climb a tree to build a house in it.

## What Do Trees Do?

Some trees drop all of their leaves every fall. Oaks, maples, birches, and willows are types of trees that do this.

Why do you think leaves fall off some trees? Do leaves drop off where you live? If so, when do they do it? When do they grow back?

Some trees lose their leaves for winter. Some trees keep their leaves all year long.

Some trees keep their leaves all year. Pine trees, spruce trees, and fir trees all do this. These trees have **needles.** Needles are narrow leaves.

Do you want to put your tree house in a tree that loses its leaves? Why or why not?

Some trees grow fruits or nuts. Apples and cherries are fruits that grow on trees. Pecans and almonds are nuts that grow on trees. Acorns are nuts that grow on oak trees.

Apples could hurt if they fell on you!

Where do fruits and nuts end up when they fall? What happens if they fall on people? On cars? On streets? Do you want your tree to have fruit or acorns on it?

# What Do Trees Need?

Trees give us what we need to breathe.

Trees are plants. All plants are living things. They need sunlight and air to make food.

Plants and people keep each other alive. Trees give off air that we breathe in. Trees take in air that we breathe out.

How will you build your tree house without hurting your tree?

# What Can Hurt Trees?

Insects attacked the tree below. The attackers in this picture are called tent caterpillars. They aren't the only kinds of insects that hurt trees. Sawfly galls, gypsy moths, and Asian longhorn beetles attack trees as well.

Insects are hurting this tree.

Some kinds of **fungus** can hurt trees, too. One kind causes **wilt** disease in oaks.

Sometimes a tree gets so sick that it dies. How could you find out if the tree you chose for your tree house is healthy or sick?

# Why Do Trees Have Roots?

Lots of roots help a tree stay strong.

You don't want the tree your house is in to fall down. So it needs to be strong. A tree gets strength from its roots.

Roots also help bring water and **nutrients** into trees.

Oak and maple trees have long roots. In a windstorm, what might happen to a tree with short roots?

# How Does a Tree Grow?

Which tree would you rather put your tree house in?

Trees are like children. They grow taller every year. Trees also grow wider.

Tree trunks of old trees are wider than tree trunks of young trees.

Look at these pictures. Which tree do you think is older? Which tree do you think would be best for a tree house? Why?

## Science at Work

## Loggers

Cutting trees down can help us. People use wood to make buildings, toys, and chairs. Wood comes from trees.

People who cut down trees for their wood are called loggers. Some loggers are careful to cut trees but not hurt forests.

This helps keep forests healthy. Loggers also need to know how to make trees fall safely. Do you think logging is a dangerous job?

A logger is cutting down a tree.

A saw like the one shown cut logs into these boards.

## Connecting to History

### Sawmills

A sawmill is a factory where machines cut logs into boards. Logs are tree trunks with the branches cut off.

Workers at a sawmill make boards of wood from logs. The boards can be different sizes. When the workers are done making the boards, other workers ship the boards to stores or people.

Long ago, sawmills got power from **water wheels.** Today, mills use electricity.

This big strong tree has a big strong name: General Sherman.

## Did You Know?

The largest tree in the world is a giant sequoia nicknamed General Sherman. General Sherman stands 275 feet (84 meters) tall. It is 36.5 feet (11 meters) wide. If you could lay the tree on a football field, it would be almost as long as the field. Scientists think the tree might be 2,700 years old!

Here are some reasons why each tree might be a good choice. These are called *pros.* Each tree also has some downsides, called *cons.* A good tree for a tree house should be strong, with a good shape.

### Tree 1: Oak Tree

*Pro:* An oak tree is strong and has long roots to support it.

*Cons:* Insects sometimes attack oak trees. Acorns fall from some oak trees. Falling acorns could make a mess. They will also make a lot of noise when they hit your roof. It might be too loud to sleep!

### Tree 2: Willow Tree

*Pros:* Willow trees are very pretty. The view out of your tree house window would be lovely. You could also hide your house in the tree's long leaves.

*Cons:* Willow trees have bendy branches that might not support a tree house.

### Tree 3: Maple Tree

*Pros:* A maple tree is strong. It has long roots to support it. No fruits or nuts fall from this kind of tree.

*Cons:* The Asian longhorn beetle attacks maple trees and makes them weak. You may have to find out if these beetles live in your tree.

### Tree 4: Pine Tree

*Pros:* Pine trees keep their needles all year long. That would give you some privacy.

*Cons:* Pines make sticky sap. That could make life a little messy.

You were asked to choose a tree early in this book. Have you changed your mind or are you staying with your first choice?

# Beyond the Puzzle

You chose your tree and built your tree house. You like it and want to stay and live there.

Does your plan to stay a long time change which tree you choose? Would you want to build in a young tree or an old tree? Where in the world would you like your tree to be?

Draw a picture of your perfect tree. Draw your perfect tree house in the branches. What makes your new home so great? As you have learned, there are worlds within leaves. Now you are part of those worlds.

# Glossary

**fungus:** organisms, such as mushrooms, molds, and yeasts, that feed on organic, or living matter.

**needles:** narrow leaves.

**nutrients:** substances living things need for life.

**roots:** the parts of the plant that are usually under the ground and bring water and food to the rest of the plant.

**water wheels:** wheels that use moving water to make it turn.

**wilt:** a disease in plants caused by fungi, bacteria, and other organisms.

# Further Reading

*Tree (EYE-KNOW),* by Penelope Arlon. DK Publishing, Inc., 2006.

*Winter Trees,* by Carole Gerber. Charlesbridge, 2008.

**Real Trees 4 Kids!** The Story and Science of Real Tree Farming.
http://www.realtrees4kids.org

# Additional Notes

The page references below provide answers to questions asked throughout the book. Questions whose answers will vary are not addressed.

**Page 8:** They grow in soil, they are tall, and they have bark.

**Page 10:** Children might answer that leaves fall from some trees because of wind or cold. In fact, trees shed leaves because they are not needed for food production during the winter months.

**Page 11:** They could damage cars and other things, hurt people and animals, and be dangerous to walk on.

**Page 13:** Look for galls, insects and insect damage, and fungus.

**Page 14:** It might fall over.

**Page 16:** Yes, because logs could fall on the loggers.

# Index